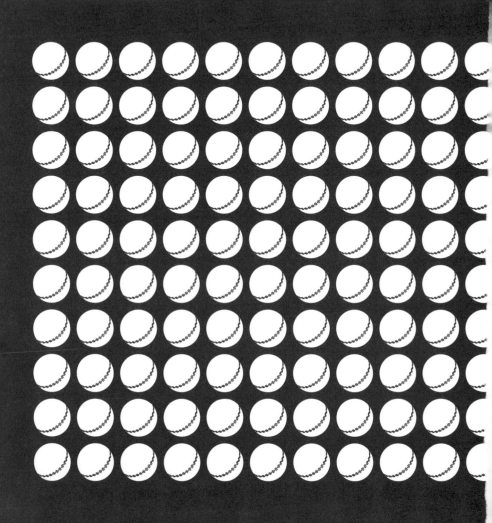

CRICKET

LET'S GET QUIZZICAL

GWION PRYDDERCH

SUMMERSDALE PUBLISHERS LTD
46 WEST STREET
CHICHESTER
WEST SUSSEX
PO19 1RP
UK

WWW.SUMMERSDALE.COM
PRINTED AND BOUND IN CHINA
ISBN: 978-1-84953-613-4

THIS PAIR ONLY APPEARS ONCE
ON THE OPPOSITE PAGE

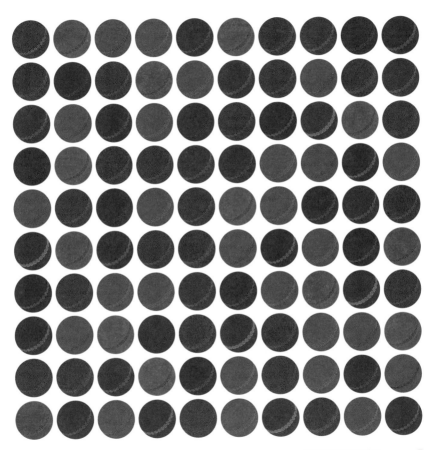

IF EVERY BATSMAN IN A CRICKET TEAM GETS BOWLED OUT FIRST BALL, WHICH NUMBER BATSMAN REMAINS 'NOT OUT'?

A) BATSMAN NUMBER 3

B) BATSMAN NUMBER 8

C) BATSMAN NUMBER 11

CRICKET KIT

GLOVES
STUMPS
PADS
BAILS
BOX
BAT
BALL
HELMET
WHITES
THIGH PAD

```
M B N W A T Y M S B
L I X W O U X V D P
B O T H I G H P A D
B A E I C D E S P X
S I M T H G T F G G
P J L E K S A L F L
M N E S D L B M L O
U O H C P I X R L V
T S O T U A V W A E
S N X Y R B S T B S
```

IN 1996 HASAN RAZA FROM PAKISTAN BECAME THE YOUNGEST CRICKETER TO MAKE HIS DEBUT IN TEST CRICKET. HOW OLD WAS HE?

A) 14 YEARS AND 227 DAYS OLD

B) 15 YEARS AND 23 DAYS OLD

C) 15 YEARS AND 358 DAYS OLD

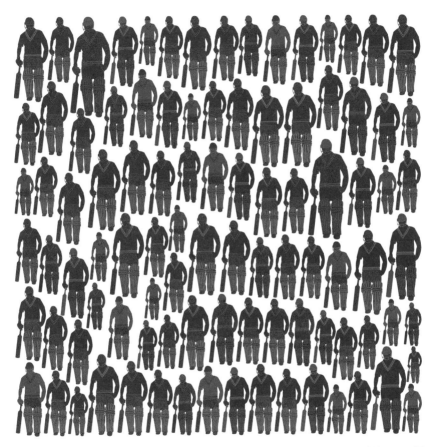

WHAT MATERIAL IS THE INSIDE OF A CRICKET BALL MADE OF?

A) RUBBER

B) CORK

C) PLASTIC

THIS PAIR ONLY APPEARS ONCE
ON THE OPPOSITE PAGE

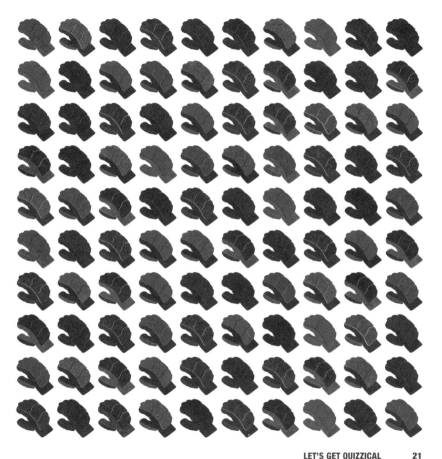

THIS PAIR ONLY APPEARS ONCE
ON THE OPPOSITE PAGE

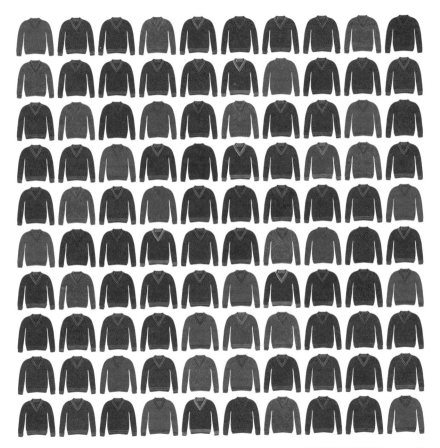

WHICH ANIMAL STOPPED PLAY BY WANDERING ONTO THE PITCH IN THE GLOUCESTERSHIRE V. DERBYSHIRE 1957 MATCH?

A) A RABBIT

B) A DOG

C) A HEDGEHOG

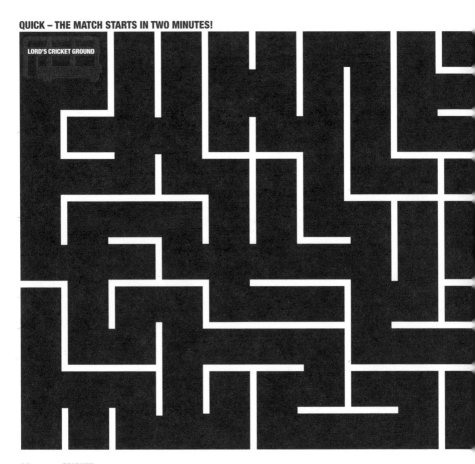

LORD'S CRICKET GROUND

KNOW YOUR
STROKES?

WHICH UNUSUAL EVENT TOOK PLACE AT LORD'S CRICKET GROUND IN 1802?

A) A STREAKER RAIDED THE PITCH FOR THE FIRST TIME

B) A BALLOONIST MADE HIS ASCENT FROM THE GROUND

C) A PARTY OF NUNS HAD A PICNIC ON THE PITCH

SPOT THE DIFFERENCE – THERE'S ONLY ONE!

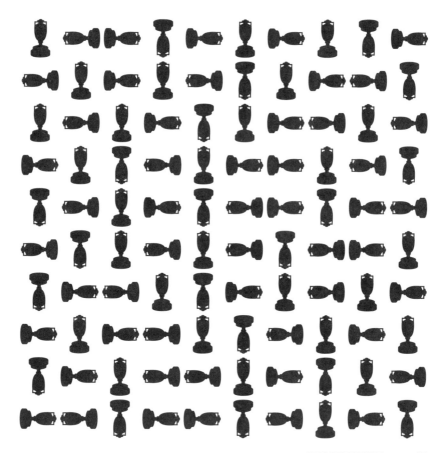

LADIES' CHANGING ROOM ▶

THE FIRST WOMEN'S TEST CRICKET MATCH WAS PLAYED BETWEEN ENGLAND AND AUSTRALIA. WHEN DID IT TAKE PLACE?

A) 1915–16

B) 1934–35

C) 1946–47

BAT NO	TOT	BAT NO
EXTRAS	WKTS	OVERS
LAST MAN		P'SHIP
LAST WKT		

BAT NO   TOT   BAT NO

EXTRAS   WTKS   OVERS

LAST MAN   P'SHIP
LAST WKT

WHO WAS THE FIRST PERSON TO SCORE A CENTURY IN A T20 INTERNATIONAL MATCH?

A) CHRIS GAYLE

B) SHAUN POLLOCK

C) ELTON CHIGUMBURA

**THIS PAIR ONLY APPEARS ONCE
ON THE OPPOSITE PAGE**

LEG-BYE   **OUT**   **NO BALL**   **SHORT RUN**

BOUNDARY 6　　　**BYE**　　　**WIDE**　　　**NEW BALL**

IT'S THE LAST BALL OF THE MATCH AND YOU'RE 5 RUNS BEHIND!

**THIS PAIR ONLY APPEARS ONCE
ON THE OPPOSITE PAGE**

EDEN (PARK) (NEW ZEALAND)

THE OVAL (ENGLAND)

SABINA (PARK) (JAMAICA)

LORD'S (ENGLAND)

CARISBROOK (NEW ZEALAND)

ELLIS (PARK) (SOUTH AFRICA)

SOPHIA (GARDENS) (WALES)

SAHARA (PARK) (SOUTH AFRICA)

EDGBASTON (ENGLAND)

GREEN (PARK) (INDIA)

```
E A Y L A S I B P K
L H G F I E E D O C
L O G I H D D O J L
I P R O P G R E N M
S A E D O B T U N V
R N E S S A H A R A
O I N I I S E A Y W
U B R F I T O N J O
R A T H E O V A L N
C S T E I N H G S E
```

WHICH OF THE THREE ANSWERS BELOW ISN'T A FIELDING POSITION?

A) SILLY MID-OFF

B) FINE LEG

C) RIGHT BACK

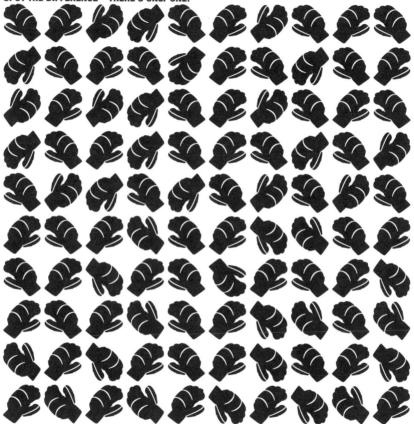

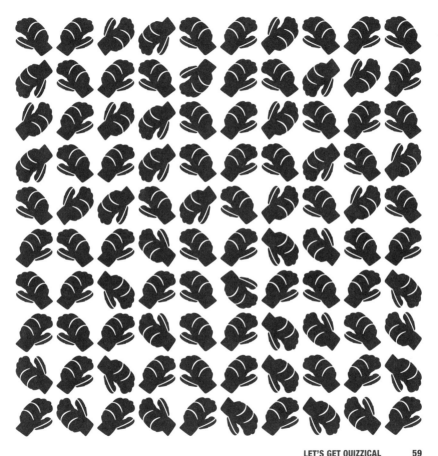

WELCOME TO THE ANAGRAM HALL OF FAME – CAN YOU WORK OUT WHO'S MADE IT?

NORMAL BAND DAD

**AUSTRALIAN
BATSMAN**

GRASSY ROBE

**WEST INDIAN
ALL-ROUNDER**

RAINS VIVID ARCH

**WEST INDIAN
BATSMAN**

HI RANK MAN

**PAKISTANI
ALL-ROUNDER**

HIM ONA BAT

**ENGLISH
ALL-ROUNDER**

ENILL LINSEED

**AUSTRALIAN
FAST BOWLER**

ELS JAIL QUACKS

**SOUTH AFRICAN
ALL-ROUNDER**

DIVED AND A JAM

**PAKISTANI
BATSMAN**

HE EARNS WAN

**AUSTRALIAN
SPIN BOWLER**

MASK WAR AIM

**PAKISTANI
ALL-ROUNDER**

RAN AIR LAB

**WEST INDIAN
BATSMAN**

TRICKING PONY

**AUSTRALIAN
BATSMAN**

THIS PAIR ONLY APPEARS ONCE
ON THE OPPOSITE PAGE

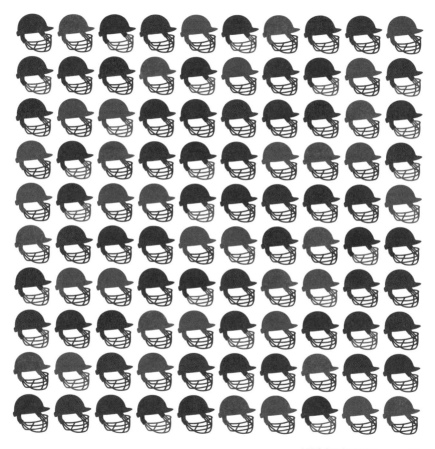

THE BATSMAN'S EDGED IT AND YOU'RE AT SLIP!

BETWEEN WHICH TWO COUNTRIES WAS THE FIRST EVER T20 INTERNATIONAL PLAYED?

A) AUSTRALIA AND NEW ZEALAND

B) KENYA AND ZIMBABWE

C) ENGLAND AND SRI LANKA

PICK THE UMPIRE OUT OF THE PILE OF JERSEYS AND HATS

BOWLER

KEEPER

SLIP

GULLY

POINT

COVER

THIRD MAN

FINE LEG

MID-WICKET

MID-OFF

SQUARE LEG

```
B N Y N A G W Y U G
P M C A D E E S F E
L I I M H L R L G L
Y D A D R E E I M E
L O M R W N V P R R
L T H I G I O I E A
U N I H D F C J P U
G I M T L O K K E Q
B O W L E R F N E S
N P O P R S T F K T
```

WHERE IS THE ORIGINAL ASHES URN KEPT?

A) MCC MUSEUM AT LORD'S IN LONDON

B) WINNER'S CRICKET GROUNDS

C) NATIONAL SPORTS MUSEUM IN AUSTRALIA

THIS PAIR ONLY APPEARS ONCE
ON THE OPPOSITE PAGE

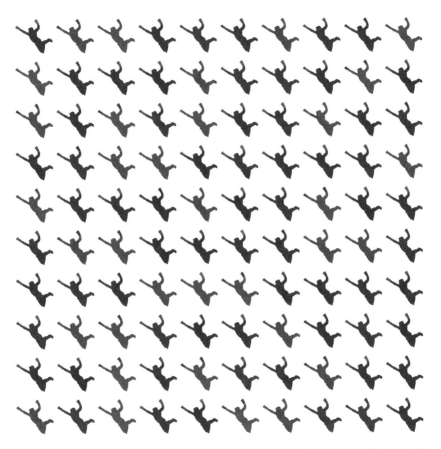

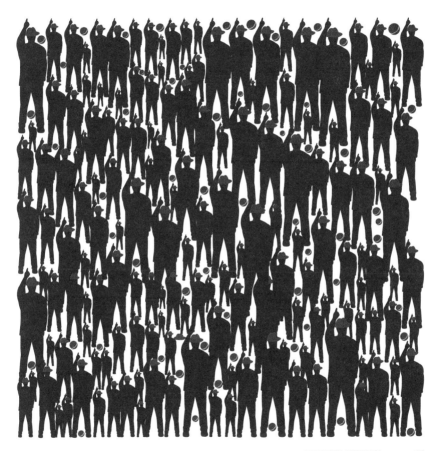

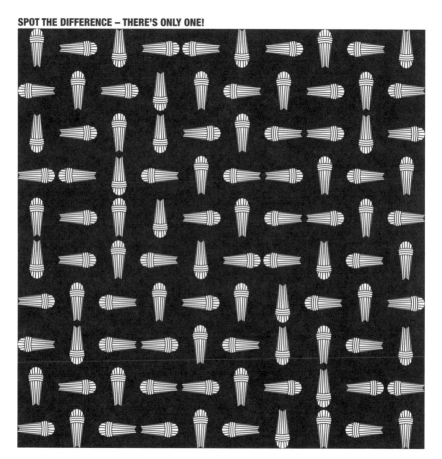

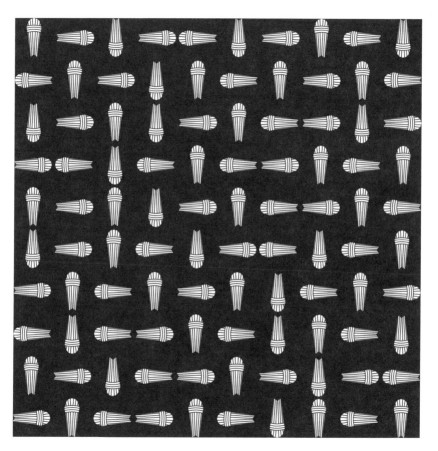

KNOW CRICKET?

1 2 3 4 5
6 7 8 9 10 11 12
13 14 15 16 17 18 19
20 21 22 23 24 25 26
27 28 29 30 31

THE LONGEST TEST MATCH IN HISTORY OCCURRED IN 1939, LASTING 14 DAYS AND FINALLY ENDING IN A TIE. WHICH TEAMS WERE PLAYING?

A) ENGLAND AND SOUTH AFRICA

B) WEST INDIES AND AUSTRALIA

C) ENGLAND AND INDIA

THIS PAIR ONLY APPEARS ONCE
ON THE OPPOSITE PAGE

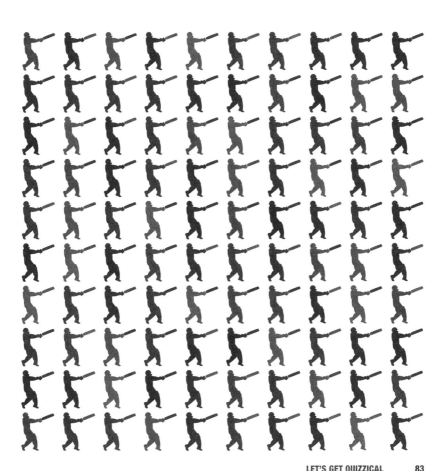

MAKE THAT STUMPING!

IN 1998 ENGLAND AND WEST INDIES PLAYED THE SHORTEST EVER TEST MATCH. HOW LONG DID IT LAST?

A) 48 MINUTES

B) 75 MINUTES

C) 93 MINUTES

SPOT THE 5 DIFFERENCES

THE ASHES

FIND THE ORANGE CRICKET BAT!

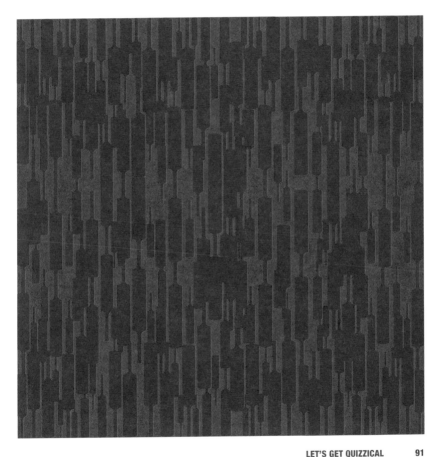

IN 1968 GARY SOBERS, PLAYING FOR NOTTINGHAMSHIRE AGAINST GLAMORGAN, BECAME THE FIRST BATSMAN TO HIT SIX SIXES IN A SINGLE OVER IN FIRST-CLASS CRICKET – WHO WAS THE WICKETKEEPER?

A) JIMMY BINKS

B) EIFION JONES

C) ALAN KNOTT

THIS PAIR ONLY APPEARS ONCE
ON THE OPPOSITE PAGE

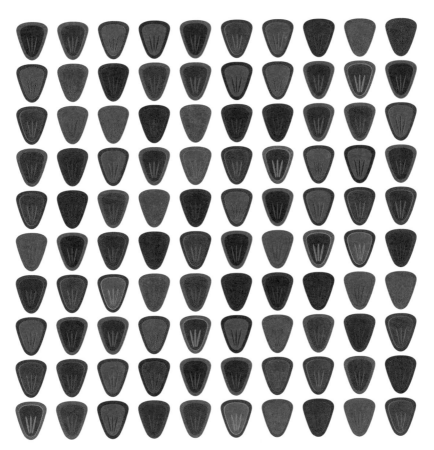

WHAT IS THE RECORD FOR THE FASTEST CRICKET BOWL?

A) 139.88 KM/H

B) 153.7 KM/H

C) 161.3 KM/H

GRACE (WILLIAM GILBERT)
LEWIS (TONY)
BOYCOTT (GEOFFREY)
GOWER (DAVID)
GATTING (MIKE)
GOOCH (GRAHAM)
LAMB (ALLAN)
STEWART (ALEC)
ATHERTON (MICHAEL)
HUSSAIN (NASSER)
STRAUSS (ANDREW)

```
G S W A B N M I M L
E D T C L E W I S A
C E F E H G H S B N
A I J C W K U O O I
R L O M N A I T Y A
G O W E R F R O C S
G A I T I E N T O S
E O S E H N C L T U
U G A T T I N G T H
W L A M B G T R S P
```

FRED TRUEMAN TURNED DOWN A PROFESSIONAL CONTRACT FROM WHICH FOOTBALL TEAM?

A) LUTON FC

B) LINCOLN CITY FC

C) WREXHAM FC

ANSWERS

P4-5

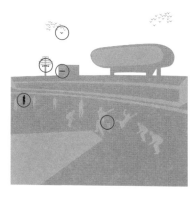

P6-7

102   CRICKET

P8-9 B) BATSMAN NUMBER 8

P10-11

P12-13 A) 14 YEARS AND 227 DAYS OLD

P14-15

P16-17

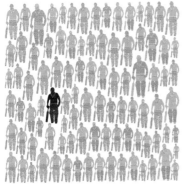

P22-23

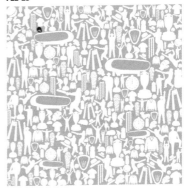

P18-19 B) CORK

P20-21

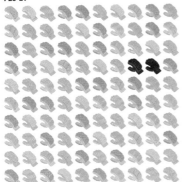

P24-25

P26-27 C) A HEDGEHOG

P28-29

P30-31

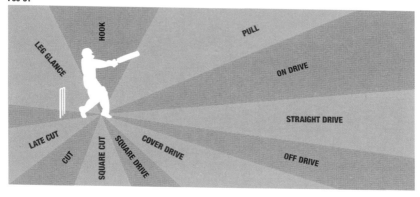

P32-33 B) A BALLOONIST MADE HIS ASCENT FROM THE GROUND

P34-35

P36-37 B) 1934–35

P38-39

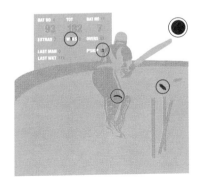

P40-41 A) CHRIS GAYLE

P42-43

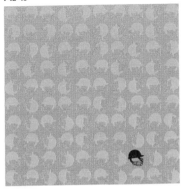

P44-45

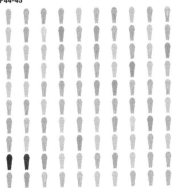

P46-47

OUT　　　NO BALL　　　BYE　　　BOUNDARY 6　　　NEW BALL　　　WIDE　　　LEG-BYE　　　SHORT RUN

P48-49

106　　CRICKET

P50-51

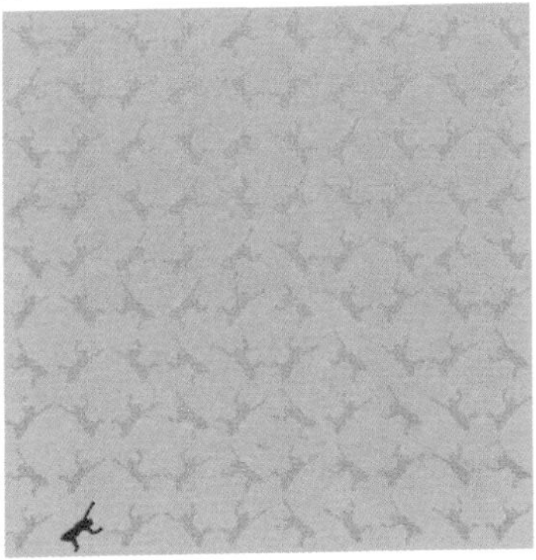

P52-53

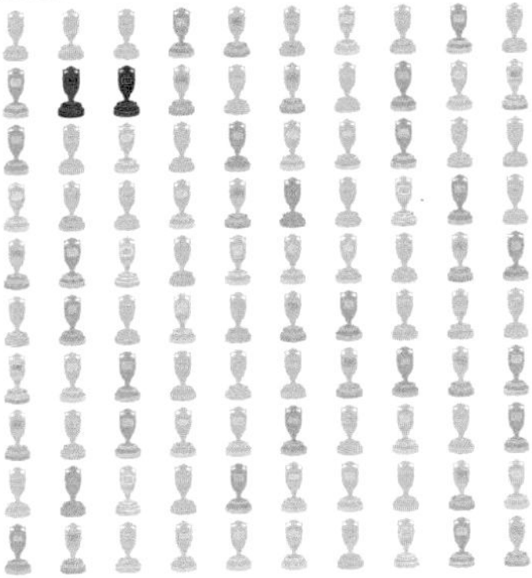

P54-55

E	A	Y	L	A	S	I	B	P	K
L	H	G	F	I	E	E	D	O	C
L	O	G	I	H	D	D	O	J	L
I	P	R	O	P	G	R	E	N	M
S	A	E	D	O	B	T	U	N	V
R	N	E	S	S	A	H	A	R	A
O	I	N	I	I	S	E	A	Y	W
U	B	R	F	I	T	O	N	J	O
R	A	T	H	E	O	V	A	L	N
C	S	T	E	I	N	H	G	S	E

P56-57 C) RIGHT BACK

P58-59

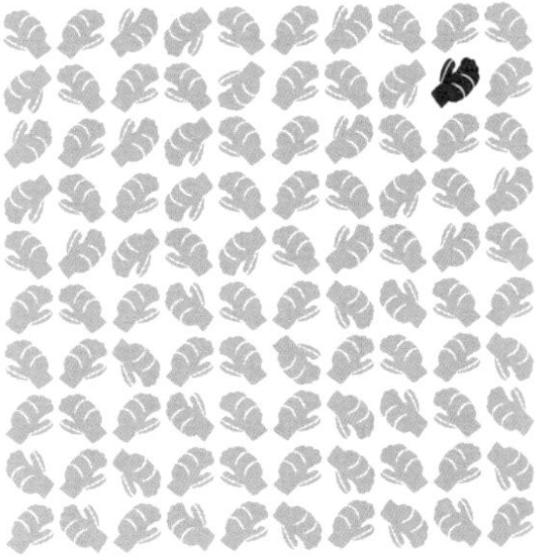

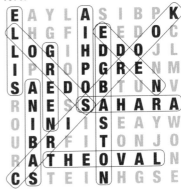

DONALD BRADMAN	GARY SOBERS	VIVIAN RICHARDS
AUSTRALIAN BATSMAN	WEST INDIAN ALL-ROUNDER	WEST INDIAN BATSMAN
IMRAN KHAN	IAN BOTHAM	DENNIS LILLEE
PAKISTANI ALL-ROUNDER	ENGLISH ALL-ROUNDER	AUSTRALIAN FAST BOWLER

JACQUES KALLIS	JAVED MIANDAD	SHANE WARNE
SOUTH AFRICAN ALL-ROUNDER	PAKISTANI BATSMAN	AUSTRALIAN SPIN BOWLER
WASIM AKRAM	BRIAN LARA	RICKY PONTING
PAKISTANI ALL-ROUNDER	WEST INDIAN BATSMAN	AUSTRALIAN BATSMAN

P66-67 A) AUSTRALIA AND NEW ZEALAND

P68-69

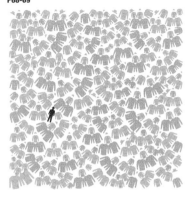

P70-71

P72-73 A) MCC MUSEUM AT LORD'S IN LONDON

P74-75

P76-77

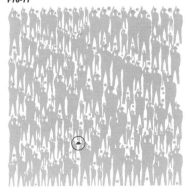

P78-79

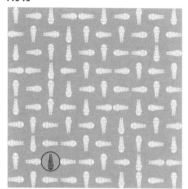

P80-81 A) ENGLAND AND SOUTH AFRICA

P82-83

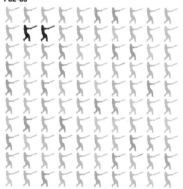

P84-85

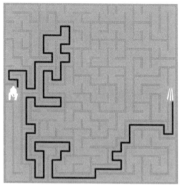

P86-87 B) 75 MINUTES

P88-89

P90-91

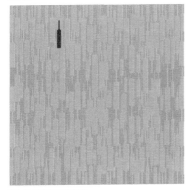

P92-93 B) EIFION JONES

P94-95

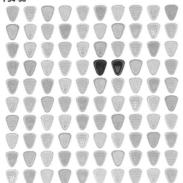

P98-99

P100-101 B) LINCOLN CITY FC

IF YOU'RE INTERESTED IN FINDING OUT MORE ABOUT OUR BOOKS, FIND US ON FACEBOOK AT SUMMERSDALE PUBLISHERS AND FOLLOW US ON TWITTER AT @SUMMERSDALE.

WWW.SUMMERSDALE.COM